This book belo

To our children, Grayson and Ella:

A moment of mindfulness
can take you miles.

THOUGHTFUL BOTS ©

MY
MINDFUL
ROBOT

Written by Joey and Melanie Acker
Illustrated by Joey Acker

Mindfulness is when your mind is in a calm place.

When you practice mindfulness, you feel in control of your emotions and body. Your mind is ready to think and learn.

Being mindful is a great feeling!

When we practice mindfulness, we are taking care of our mind, heart, and body.

Mind

Body

Heart

When we practice mindfulness, it can help us when we are feeling anxious, angry, or overwhelmed.

You can practice mindfulness as soon as you notice you are getting upset. It can help you avoid feeling like you are going to explode.

You can be mindful by taking a walk with an adult, or by going to a safe, quiet place.

You can be mindful by writing your feelings in a journal, or by listening to music that helps you feel calm.

You can be mindful by slowly taking big breaths, making sure to breathe in through your nose and breathe out through your mouth.

Six ideas to use at home or school:

- Talk to your child or student about strategies to use for mindfulness. Practice them together, so the child will be prepared when it's necessary to use them.

- Create a safe, quiet place in your home or classroom and designate it as a Mindful Space.

- Practice mindful breathing (taking deep breaths in through your nose and out through your mouth).

- Keep a journal handy for writing about feelings - or have paper and pen, crayons, or markers available for making drawings about feelings.

- Together, practice mindful breathing and stretching.

- Celebrate when they use their strategies!!

Melanie Acker, MS is a Licensed Professional Counselor. She has experience as an elementary teacher, school counselor, administrator and parent. Melanie is an advocate for social emotional learning.

She enjoys sharing the power of emotions and strategies to help children and adults. The goal of the Thoughtful Bots series is to teach children about emotions and how to handle them in a kid-friendly, simple way.

Joey Acker, M.Ed has worked with children ages 4-13 in daycares and public schools. He has experience as an elementary teacher, administrator, and parent.

Joey is passionate about teaching and reinforcing strategies for children to grow and manage their emotions. He enjoys co-writing and illustrating the Thoughtful Bots and Wonder Who Crew series.

Made in United States
Troutdale, OR
02/03/2025

28618868R00021